REAL FISHERMEN NEVER LIE

by
John Davis

PINEGROVE
PUBLISHING

PO Box 557 • Winona Lake, IN 46590

Dedicated With Love To
My Daughter Debbie

Also by John Davis, *Real Fishermen Are Never Thin*, 123 pp.
$7.95 from Pinegrove Publishing, P.O. Box 557, Winona Lake,
IN 46590.

First printing — Oct., 1993
Second printing — Dec., 1993

Published by   Pinegrove Publishing
                P.O. Box 557
                Winona Lake, IN 46590 USA

ISBN 0-9635865-1-3

TABLE OF CONTENTS

The Ol' Scribe at Work

Introduction

I like fishermen.

They possess, among other things, endless patience, enormous creativity and unchallengeable dedication. It has been my privilege to live around hunters and fishermen from my earliest days.

Two of the finest outdoor people in my life have been my parents, who both love to fish. I cherish fond memories of boyhood days filled with fishing trips to the south Jersey shores where we battled stripers in the surf and flounder in the bays.

The last 34 years of my life, however, have been spent in the small mid-western town of Warsaw, Indiana. Rich in history and tradition, this city is surrounded by more than 100 lakes, all of which provide superb fishing.

It is a town of celebrities and characters which are, at times, difficult to distinguish.

A small store in the center of town has served as a gathering place for just about every type of male

1

species that walks this earth. Known as Breadings' Cigar Store, it boasts a cultural diversity that would make a modern sociologist drool.

This small restaurant is a hangout for judges, lawyers, farmers, salesmen, educators and just regular people.

Dominoes is the game of choice, but games are regularly interrupted by lively debates over everything from socks to saints. Its unique character has caught the attention of CBS television as well as various Indiana newspapers.

In the following pages you will find frequent references to the eatery and its unflappable chef— Burleigh Burgh. Co-owner, Craig Smith, adds a touch of sanity to this food emporium, known more for its bedlam than its burgers.

I hope the unique perspective and quiet charm of Warsaw as reflected in the stories that follow, will spark the kind of curiosity that might even bring you here for a visit.

This book is an edited collection of various "Outdoor Scene" columns that have appeared in the *Warsaw Times Union* during the past 13 years.

Many folks have helped me with this little volume. Frank Benyousky, Assistant Professor of Communications at Grace College, did a superb job of editing as did Joel Curry, Community Relations Director at Kosciusko Community Hospital.

Eldon Kibbey, President of Environment Control Building Maintenance Company of Indianapolis, Inc., corrected the galley proofs with his usual care for detail.

Kevin Carter, professional artist and marketing specialist, prepared the illustrations, and Brenda Minard was responsible for typesetting and page design. I express my sincere gratitude to all the above individuals who have made this project so enjoyable.

My passionate desire is that as you read this book, you will enjoy a hearty laugh or two and with that, will be able to forget, a least for a moment, the pressures that surround you every day.

It Was This Big!

Real Fishermen Never Lie

There is a nasty and persistent rumor out there that all anglers are liars.

My friend, Harvy Fern, puts it this way: "Fishermen never tell the truth. The fish is always bigger than it really is, the battle to pull it in longer, and the bait smaller."

"When they don't catch a fish, lies are even more abundant," he insists.

This is, of course, a very serious charge, which, if accurate, hangs like a dark cloud over the head of every person whoever dunked a worm, including Izaak Walton, many American presidents, seven of Jesus' disciples and more than 62 million fishermen in the United States.

I suspect that the problem, however, exists not in the way an angler tells his or her story, but in the manner that the story is heard and interpreted by those lacking literary depth and diversity.

What we outdoor types face is a serious and

substantial public shortfall in literary sophistication, biological scholarship and cultural sensitivity.

When, for example, Wilber Wormwood tells the gang at Breadings' Cigar Store that he caught a 28-inch, eight-pound bass in Winona Lake, which only measured 26-inches and weighed six pounds when his wife checked it at home, there are those who will erroneously conclude he has tampered with the truth.

What they don't recognize is that fish shrink and lose weight through dehydration when they are out of the water for an extended period of time. The issue here is biological change, not statistical prevarication!

Blessed with creative imaginations and literary inventiveness, fishermen do tend to describe their angling exploits in vivid and dramatic terms.

However, let me be clear. No fisherman worth his salt would wish to reshape reality beyond reasonable recovery. The true angler only uses the techniques of poetic embellishment to add literary richness to his fishing stories.

We call this "poetic license." For example, Fred Flatbottom hooked onto a giant northern in Lake Wawasee, and as he eased the monster up to the boat he exclaimed, "Hey, this fish has only one eye."

"Don't get excited," his partner, Buddy Splitshot, shouted, "the other eye is under this side of the boat."

Any dummy can say, "I caught a big fish on Lake Wawasee." The literary bankruptcy of this statement is self-evident. But it takes a special intellectual creativity to describe the fish the way Buddy did.

Then there is "verbal innovation." This, too, is often mistaken for lying.

Zeke Barnstorm of Fogbottom, Kentucky is good

at this form of storytelling. He is one of the best bass anglers in the region and has been unusually successful in protecting his secret methods. When asked by a group of frustrated anglers how he so consistently landed bass five pounds or larger, he responded nonchalantly, "I use the Red Man Chewing Tobacco method."

"I toss some tobacco on the water and let the bass eat it. When they come up to spit, I hit them over the head with an oar."

Now, whether this is the truth or yet another sophisticated equivocation is still debated around the pot-belled stove at the downtown hardware store. Whatever you call it, you have to admit that the story is terrifically innovative and, therefore, of unique literary worth.

Della Hucklemeyer's account of how they had to back a tow truck up to the water to pull her catfish in, also falls into the category of verbal innovation.

Another highly complicated and subtle literary device used by fishermen is "prose modification." This type of storytelling has frequently been mistaken for lying by intellectually shallow computer types who think that mathematical precision is the warp and woof of life.

What is often overlooked is that classical literature is filled with numerical estimations, statistical hyperbole and rounded numbers. In the same way that generals on the field of battle cannot take the time to precisely count the enemy soldiers who escape, so also are anglers, who battle a large bass in turbulent water and lose it, compelled to approximate the size of the fish.

For example, Buster Chops tells about his fight with a giant bluegill on Winona Lake as follows:

"Ah was doodle-socken in a winder in some garbage at the south end of the lake when a 'gill smashed mah bait. Ah battled it fer two hours, but it busted the line and got away. It musta gone at least three pounds."

This rich use of the English language might well be suspected by angling cynics as an intentional distortion of the truth.

Actually Buster was describing how he was jigging a lure in an opening in the vegetation at the south end of Winona Lake when a very large bluegill took his bait.

A furious battle ensued, and with water splashing and weeds whirling he was compelled to estimate what the fish's size was, based on its fight and a very quick glimpse of its body.

Numerical hyperbole is required here to capture the intense battle that the fish waged. Most knowledgeable and perceptive anglers would immediately recognize that this is what the fish "seemed" to weigh when all factors were taken into consideration.

"Environmental fabrication" is also a highly developed literary device employed by anglers world-wide. A fish might have been caught during very adverse weather conditions, and to properly reflect that fact, and round out the story, additional dramatic details must be employed.

For example, Melvin Mossback caught a large crappie during very strong winds. To underscore the challenging nature of these conditions he prefaced his story with, "Da wind was so strong dat a hen on shore got turned around da wrong way and laid the same egg three times."

This environmental fabrication adds color and tone to the story that is necessary if we are to distinguish one great fishing story from another.

Of course, it goes without saying that if a sportsman's nose grows longer each time he tells a fish story, you know he's not a real fisherman, but a pretender.

Real fishermen might indulge in poetic license, verbal innovation or prose modification, but lie? Never!

That practice is reserved for politicians.

Man's Best Friend

In The Dog House

The whole mess was downright embarrassing.

I had just acquired a young English setter for pheasant hunting, and was taking him to the woods to begin his field training.

Along the way we met two nasty German shepherds, and before I knew what was happening all three dogs turned on me. It seemed they thought it would be fun to see how fast I could run and how well I could climb a tree.

They had to be impressed with my efforts in both these areas. For less dedicated hunters this kind of incident would have gotten the mutt a one-way ticket back to the pet shop.

But this was a good-looking setter and the owner had assured me he came from a good line of hunting dogs, so we carried on.

After he had a few days to adjust to his new home, I decided it was time for him to get used to the noise of a shotgun. At 14 years of age, I was not too conscious of how very sensitive a dog's hearing is.

We traveled a short distance from my home and I fired my single barrel, 20 gauge shotgun. The dog really made a slick move...three feet straight up! When he hit the ground, all four feet were motoring at 40 miles an hour, and he headed straight for the house. My neighbor thought it was hilarious, but I was mortified.

Things finally did get ironed out, however, and "Topper," as I called him, turned out to be a superb field dog.

Man's dedication to these humble beasts is nicely captured by the poetic pen of Claypool's own Dork Goodflat:

Breathes there a man with a soul so dead,
Who never to himself has said,
I may be poor and live in a hut,
But I'd sell my soul for a mangy mutt.

It has been said that a dog is an intelligent four-footed animal who walks around with some dope on the end of his leash.

Dog owners certainly do take their relationship with those furry little creatures very seriously. Just observe how much care is taken to give the right name to the dog. Fido and Rover are generally out these days, but look for Meg, Sara, Lucy or Carla. Other titles include Max, Buffy, Pepper, Lady, Bear, Patches, Lucky, King, Brandy and Blackie.

Food names are also in vogue. Listen carefully and you will hear such tags as Pizza, Cheddar, Noodles, Jam, Cupcake, Butterscotch, Honey, Chocolate Chip, Snickers, Peaches, and Cream Puff.

This naming business has given gigantic headaches to Warsaw paramedics and firemen. When a hysterical lady calls and says, "Lucy just ran away," they are not sure whether they should bring a net or call the missing persons bureau.

During my college days, I was working part-time for a private ambulance service and was called to a house that had been struck by a fuel truck.

While my assistant was attending the driver of the truck, I checked the lady who had run from the house screaming. Fire had engulfed more than 30 percent of the dwelling by the time we arrived.

"Please go in and get Charlie," she begged. "Where's your son located," I asked. "It's not my boy, it's my dog, and he's in the kitchen," she sobbed. I crawled into the kitchen and brought Charlie out, much to her relief. With a dramatically quieter voice she then said, "Oh, yes, somebody should go into the enclosed porch because my husband is asleep there."

Now friends, there's a man with some marriage challenges!

While many dogs are content with their domestic environments, I suspect that most would probably rather be working for the fire department than lying around the house. They betray this secret desire by the way they constantly scout around for hydrants.

Fireside chats or stove-side conversations among duck hunters will always produce some interesting tales about hunting dogs.

Pierceton's Ezra Beatleman recalls his attempted sale of "Blackie," a lab retriever that moved so efficiently it walked on water to get a downed duck!

"I had this city slicker from Fort Wayne who wanted to buy my dog, so we took Blackie out for a field trial. This guy shot down a duck and, as usual, the dog skimmed across the top of the water and recovered the mallard," Ezra recalled.

"Well, what do you think about ol' Blackie?" Ezra asked the man.

"Oh, he's a good dog, all right, but I don't want him. The crazy thing can't even swim," he responded.

Jack Woodslab recalls the difficulty he had hunting ducks in the small ponds and lakes in Kosciusko County. Finally, he got a dog trained to sneak up to the ponds and then return to him scratching the ground to indicate how many ducks were on the water. If there were five ducks, his dog would scratch five times.

One weekend he loaned ol' Red to his friend, Sam Splitshot. Within hours Sam returned with the dead carcass of Red. "We were hunting at a small pond near Leesburg; when Red returned, he was jumping, scratching the ground and frothing at the mouth," he explained.

"While whining, he grabbed a dead limb in his mouth and was thrashing it about violently," he continued. "We thought he had gone mad, so we shot him."

"He wasn't mad," Jake responded with irritation. "He was simply trying to tell you there were more ducks on that lake than you could shake a stick at!"

Coon hunting is a favorite sport in the county and the stories about coon dogs are infinite. Barry Busbrack of Atwood, was getting up in years and, with failing eyesight, was not able to go coon hunting anymore. Hit with a stroke of genius, he bought a monkey and trained it, once the dog had located a coon, to climb a tree and shoot the coon.

Well, it seemed the dog located what he thought was a coon, and the monkey raced up the tree but did not return for 15 minutes. No shots were fired and no monkey was seen.

Finally, the monkey came down from the tree and shot the dog. "One thing that monkey does not like is a lying dog," Barry explained with a sly grin.

Hector Lebble of Packerton claims he had the greatest 'possum dog that ever lived. "That dog was so good at catching 'possum, all you had to do was get a skinnin' board the size you wanted, and the dog would bring in a 'possum to fit the board," he bragged.

"One day my wife left her ironing board outside the door. That dog left home and we haven't seen him since. He's still looking for a 'possum to fit that board," Hector said.

As an outdoor writer, I always felt a sense of safety writing about dogs because they cannot read or write. At least, I can't recall getting any correspondence from Fido! But their owners can be a bit testy at times.

I landed in the proverbial dog house not long ago when I suggested to a lady that her mutt needed some attention and should not be left to roam the streets day after day.

"Listen, you smotsch," she shouted as she passed me on Warsaw's Center Street. "You can just be glad I didn't let Max bite you a moment ago when he growled. He doesn't particularly like outdoor writers, you know."

"Well, I'm glad you finally see it my way and have decided to keep the dog in check," I responded.

"See it your way, my foot," she snapped back with righteous anger. "I just didn't want him to bite you, and then die of food poisoning..."

This Is Fun?

Fishing
Is Not Fun

I'm not really crazy about flying.

My sentiments have nothing to do with United's friendly skies, but everything to do with sterile airports, constant delays, concourses that span three counties, and boring conversations.

The one bright spot in this otherwise bleak scenario is what I like to call "social roulette." You never know who will be assigned to the seat next to you by the all-wise airline computer system.

Not long ago, a lady in her 30's slid by me to take her place next to the window. She was smartly decked out in a dark gray, pin-striped suit with a wide, burgundy striped tie.

After she was comfortably situated, I began reading one of my favorite fishing magazines to help me survive yet another four-hour flight. (For you critical types who think I should be poring over things more profound and intellectually exhilarating, I should inform you that I read *War and Peace, The*

Source and Augustine's *The City of God* while waiting for my delayed flight to take off.)

Call it instinct, if you will, but I had an uneasy feeling about this gal and wondered if the airline had dealt me another bad hand.

"Hello, I'm Fozzy Farleft (not her real name, of course). Is that a fishing magazine?" she asked, while glancing at the publication in my weather-worn hands.

"Why, yes it is," I responded. "I'm an outdoor writer and fisherman. I enjoy reading about the great outdoors."

"Well, I mean no personal offense, but I regard outdoor writers as exploitative and barbaric bozos. Fishing is nothing more than the murder of innocent creatures just so the angler can have some fun. This is a most despicable enterprise in an enlightened age," she concluded with her pious, unpowdered nose probing the stratosphere.

No fear about a boring conversation here, boys and girls!

"I'm sorry you feel that way about fishing. My wife and I both enjoy this sport and find the fillets to be very good eating."

"Oh, so you're married, too," she concluded with somewhat belligerent tones. "I'm glad I'm enlightened and don't need to marry. It is nothing more than legalized rape, anyway."

My keen outdoor writer's instincts told me that we had a lively one on the end of the verbal line, and I was more than ready for a little battle activity.

"The whole problem with your philosophical outlook, Fozzy, is that you don't know anything about fishing," I announced calmly. "Contrary to what you may have concluded, fishing is not fun."

"Do you really think getting up at 4:00 a.m., drinking a black brew that would pass for embalming fluid, driving 10 miles in the fog, waiting 25 minutes for your partner to get dressed, and discovering the bait shop is out of nightcrawlers is fun?"

"Then, there are the inevitable rope burns you get while putting your boat in the water on a very steep ramp. Throughout the morning mosquitoes remove pints of your best corpuscles, both red and white."

Now I was really getting warmed up and rolling.

I looked into her bloodshot eyes and continued with pontifical authority and no small amount of exuberance.

"Fun? You really think fishing for a few ounces of fillets is fun? I spend a whole day getting shishkebabbed in the blazing sun, and the soggy sandwich I stored in my tackle box tastes like dried bait and dead fish. To round out the agony, my trolling motor battery regularly dies just when the bass start hitting 50 feet from the boat."

"I won't even begin to talk about the cost for this thrill-a-minute activity because I might break out in tears," I concluded with proper sincerity.

"Enough talk about my hobbies, what kind of special interests do you have?" I inquired.

"I enjoy growing different kinds of roses," she responded in subdued and civil tones. "Then, I cut them and make various arrangements for my friends. It's all really very enjoyable."

"Oh, Fozzy, that won't do. I'm shocked and devastated at this very disturbing news," I groaned.

"Now, let me get this straight," I continued. "You feed these little plants until they produce majestic flowers, then in the prime of life, you chop the innocent roses off just so you can have fun making bouquets and arrangements?"

She gazed back at me in speechless shock.

"Nothing personal, mind you, but I regard such activity as quite immoral and unfair. At least my fish have a choice, and they are able to swim away from my offerings. The poor rose has no alternatives and it cannot flee. Its fate will be to face rapid deterioration and an inglorious burial in a garbage can just so you can have some fun."

"That's not fair," she protested. "Roses don't live consciously like animals and fish do, so they don't feel anything."

"Ah, but they do have feelings. Friends of mine play symphony music in their homes for their plants to enjoy. They insist that the plants, roses included, grow better with music and will, at times, even lean in the direction of the music," I noted with authority. "Plants are living beings with feelings although they might not be able to scream when you snip them in the prime of life."

"I guess there's not much we agree on" she observed coldly.

"Oh, I don't know. How do you feel about Bill Clinton's health care plan, the values and the future of the National Organization of Women, education, religious cults, abortion on demand or the Chicago Cubs?"

There was no answer. Fozzy just stared into space with glassy eyes.

That issue of the fishing magazine was particularly good, I might add.

The Serious Dieter

The Outdoor
Diet Plan

Tired of having to go to a grain elevator to get weighed? Is flab frustrating you? Is "thin" only a dim and distant desire?

Then, the ol' scribe has a perfect diet for you.

For years now I have battled bulges and fought fat without one significant victory to my credit—that is, until the startling discovery of the complete outdoor diet plan.

Actually, I can't take credit for all the system because I originally got the idea from Kermit the Frog, who visited Warsaw a few weeks back to assess the possibility of running for mayor in the next city election.

After discussing the complexities of Warsaw politics, Kermit and I turned our attentions to dieting.

To start things off, Kermit challenged me with the question, "Have you ever seen a fat frog?" Of course, I hadn't. I was stunned by the power of his observation. What was their secret?! I had to know the answer to this critical biological fact.

Kermit's answer was simple, "They do it the outdoor way."

The plan could not have come at a better time for me. So bad was my situation that I was walking through doors sideways, and feeling totally stymied by shoes that required tying.

I had even resorted to reading the new book, *The Body Pavarotti*. Sure, I tried other systems in an attempt to recover a figure which only required a 30-inch belt to hold up slim Levi's.

There was the grapefruit diet, the banana and milk diet, the hay diet, the watermelon diet, the protein diet, the tea and crackers diet, the rice diet and the fruit diet, to name just a few.

Harvy Moot had a great idea for me a year ago—the Dr. Stillman diet in which you drink a minimum of eight glasses of water a day. "Why, I lost three pounds in one day," Harvy bragged.

I found out later that he lost three pounds in one day because his bladder fell out.

Thorndike Thistlefoot tried to talk me into his all new harmonica diet. This plan allows you only to eat foods you can suck through the holes of a harmonica.

The tranquilizer diet was suggested to me by Arnie Adenoid. "You won't lose any weight with this diet, but it doesn't bother you if you are fat," he explained.

Henry Hornripple, whom I have out-fished on my past three visits to Winona Lake, suggested I try the new lo-cal hair tonic. "It's especially designed for fatheads," he informed me.

I thought I had the problem licked when I went to Freddie's Fat Farm in Claypool. But the 10-mile hikes, and four-hour exercise periods followed by a glass of prune juice had me talking to the dead flies in my room's ceiling lamp, so I decided to bail out of the joint. Six months in A.A. (Appetites Anonymous) didn't seem to help either.

So all you plump pedestrians, beefy businesspersons, stocky students, portly professors, obese office workers, corpulent councilmen, and pudgy principals make use of what follows and your troubles will be over!

The following diet system is the result of two years of research conducted by three Warsaw witch doctors and Kermit the Frog. Consult your doctor and psychiatrist before embarking on this plan, however. It is not for every tenderfoot!

Monday

    Breakfast — One ounce fresh prune juice (gargle only).

    Lunch — Two ounces of Winona Lake algae and one ounce of plankton.

    Dinner - Squid McNuggets, one ounce of dandelion greens, one glass of dehydrated water.

Tuesday

    Breakfast — Two freshwater shrimp antennae (no salt added).

    Lunch — One dish of sauerkraut-flavored jello.

    Dinner — One ounce of muskrat nose with a dash of chili pepper; dessert: one dip of spinach ripple ice cream; one glass of dehydrated water.

Wednesday

    Breakfast — Three lightly toasted blackberry

seeds.

Lunch — Mosquito knuckles and four broasted bluegill dorsal fins.

Dinner — Cream of tadpole soup, one glass of dehydrated water.

Thursday

Breakfast — Pickled hummingbird tongue.

Lunch — One char-broiled algae burger.

Dinner — Bicuspid of horse (two ounces), one glass of dehydrated water.

Friday

Breakfast — Two snail antennae.

Lunch — One cup of 'possum tail soup.

Dinner — Cricket knees with one bay leaf or one crayfish claw in mussel juice, one glass of dehydrated water.

Saturday

Breakfast — Powdered duck bill and four broiled perch fins.

Lunch — Two grains of celery seed.

Dinner — Cold camel tongue with red cayenne pepper or rump of lady bug, one glass of dehydrated water.

Sunday

Breakfast — One doughnut hole (no sugar).

Lunch — Pigeon wing with two ounces of onion and garlic cole slaw (Those with 1:30 p.m. committee meetings may want to pass up on the cole slaw).

Dinner — Catfish whiskers sauteed in Walnut Creek water (adds a nice oily touch), one glass of dehydrated water with a slice of lemon (this addition to the daily drink is a celebration of success in surviving the diet).

Those of you who are about to embark on this exciting slim-down adventure, please remember that abstinence is always more painful than indigestion. It is not the way you keep your weight down that really matters, only the will to do so.

While this fabulous diet plan might look frivolous to the superficial observer, remember that 13 million frogs and three witch doctors can't all be wrong.

Rosebud Makes Her Point

It's A Matter
of Definition

"I want some answers and I want them now," Rosebud Hornripple thundered, with her 230-pound frame more than adequately filling the back door at Breadings' Cigar Store.

"You and ol' fishnose (her husband, Barney) spent more than $1,300 on your recent angling jaunt to Alaska, and all I've gotten out of the affair is a million dollar story and two pounds of fish fillets. And to top it all off, I just learned that those fish fillets actually came from Marsh's Supermarket, not the sparkling waters of Homer, Alaska."

"Now look, bub, I know this whole cockamamie fishing trip was your idea. I want some straight answers, or someone's facial anatomy is going to be radically rearranged," she barked while staring down the entire collection of humanity gathered at the back table.

"Rosebud, I don't know what Barney has told you about the Alaskan adventure, but I suspect the problem here is not so much in the telling of the story, as in its interpretation. Among Breadings' intellectuals it's technically known as hermeneutics, that is, the science of interpretation," I explained.

"We five-star chefs call it stripping the baloney out of the bread," chef Burleigh Burgh noted with more earthy simplicity.

Rosebud snorted indignantly.

So, in an effort to keep the ol' scribe from being flattened by this Sherman tank-like woman, I offered to help her understand the true meaning inherent in her husband's fishing lingo. Today, in order to assist wives everywhere in understanding their husband's fishing stories, I want to share that same glossary of fishing phrases that helped dear Rosebud see the light. The expressions here, come from real life fish tales and will be given with an appropriate interpretation in parentheses.

1. "You just can't beat the fresh air and exercise we had." (The motor broke down five miles from the cabin and he had to row back through high winds)

2. "It was a bit windy." (His $8.95 map and $23 compass blew overboard).

3. "That treble hook worm assembly you bought me for my birthday really had hooking and holding power." (He hooked himself in the seat of his pants, ripping the material and embedding the hooks securely in his skin. After the doctor removed them, he was not able to sit down the rest of the trip).

4. "Things really sink rapidly in clear, clean water." (He stepped off the pier with a 30-horsemotor in his hands).

5. "A lot of guys went to live bait when the action slowed, but I'm a purist. It was artificials all the way." (He didn't catch any fish)

6. "The environment was drastically different from what we normally encounter, and it can't help but affect you." (The weather was lousy and he caught a cold).

7. "It's all a matter of luck when you get to those really large lakes." (He didn't catch any fish).

8. "The fish were hanging way back in the cabomba, not doing diddly squat." (He didn't get any bites and didn't catch any fish).

9. "I missed a real hawg that would have gone six, anyway. She sucked in a ten-inch plastic worm with a chartreuse firetail and ran right at the boat so fast with it I couldn't tighten on her." (He had one hit all day on a three-inch plastic worm by a one-half pound bass and lost it).

10. "Things really got exciting out there, and I was glad I had my heart medicine along." (This is the line he used when the motor on the 20-foot boat broke down and someone had to volunteer to row it back to shore).

11. "I really prefer the little ones because they taste so much better." (He didn't get one decent sized fish the whole trip).

12. "I've just got to get some properly balanced equipment this winter to better secure directional control in my casting." (He whipped his six-foot graphite rod around in a side-arm cast and embedded a large plug

securely in the forehead of his fishing partner).

13. "We really covered the lake well even though visibility was minimal." (He got lost in a fog and rowed around in large circles half the morning).

14. "We hopped on a large charter boat in Lake Michigan, and I really had some action with the steelhead." (He got seasick and spent most of the time vomiting in the ship's lavatory).

15. "All the bass in that school we ran into were exactly the same size." (He bought his fish fillets at a supermarket).

"You see, Rosebud," I said more confidently, now that her lumpy frame was serenely positioned on a chair, "when you don't catch many fish, details aren't that important. What counts is the general aesthetic benefit one receives from just being in the great outdoors. When fish are caught, however, be prepared for a lengthy blow-by-blow account of every bite."

"Well, at least I now understand some of that jargon I get after every fishing trip," she observed, "but I am still concerned about his parting words this morning.

"He said he was off to a special lecture by Professor Burgh at Breadings' Educational Emporium on the subject of 'The Subtle Nuances of Paleolithic Pithecanthropoid Types and the Archaic Defensive Capability of the St. Louis Cardinals with Special Emphasis on Domino Sequences in National League Alignments.'"

"Rosebud, " I responded, taking great pains to keep a straight face, "there isn't a dictionary in existence that could help you with that one. Just chalk it up to cultural enrichment and let it go at that."

The Olympic Mud Sling

Election Year Olympics

The whole city of Warsaw was crackling with excitement!

Busloads of enthusiastic Democrats and Republicans cruised along Center Street toward Kosciusko Olympic Stadium, which was a blaze of color with flags from every state.

"Wow, Mayor Jeff Plank really out-did himself this time," Achish Featherbelt gurgled with pride. "Just think of it, olympic events for political candidates. Warsaw will be the talk of the nation."

Weary of dull press conferences and so-called debates where positions are presented in canned fashion, the mayor, along with Jimmy Carter, Richard Nixon, Gerald Ford, and Ronald Reagan, decided to get American politics off dead center and into an arena where substantive confrontations could take place.

More than 85,000 looked on as George Bush, riding a large elephant, led the Republican team into the stadium , while Bill Clinton, mounted on a small donkey, carried the flag for the Democrats.

Before the competition began, the crowd was entertained with a vocal solo from Dr. Robert Walkabit (the first MD to perform a hernia transplant) who gave a stirring rendition of the 1950s hit song, "The Object of My Infection."

"Gentlemen, start your events," announcer Rush Limbaugh screamed into the microphone to the delight of the crowd.

The first event was the Presidential Sled Pull. This is actually a team event where the presidential candidate attempts to pull his nominee for vice president on a wooden sled for a distance of 100 feet.

Clinton started and after huffing and puffing for a distance of 75 feet, gave up. Bush grabbed his rope and dragged Quayle for the full 100 feet. "I told you Gore was dead weight," Bob Dole shouted to the Democratic cheering section.

"That's a crock of baloney," Senator Joe Biden shot back. "All your victory proves is that Quayle is a lightweight."

Next, the attention of the crowd shifted to the north end of the stadium where the Mud Sling event was about to take place.

"Gentleman, the object of this competition is to sling as much mud at your opponent as you can in 10 minutes from 25 feet away. The one who is most coated with mud will be awarded the loser's tin medallion, while the winner will get the gold," Limbaugh explained.

The first fling came from Bush as he faced Clinton. "Jane Fonda might be liberal, but at least she went to Vietnam." Splat!

Then it was Clinton's turn: "You wouldn't even

be in this competition, you old fossil, if Barbara hadn't been spiking your Geritol with steroids." Sploosh!

Al Gore and Dan Quayle filled the air with mud and it was flying in every direction much to the delight of the Washington press corps who took up 2,376 seats on the sidelines.

Bush then stepped into the ring again and with unbelievable gusto shouted, "Under your leadership Arkansas has fallen so far behind modern education that three-fourths of your high school teachers think the English Channel is a television station." Splat!

"If it weren't for country clubs, posh restaurants and international playboys, there wouldn't be a Republican party," Clinton bellowed. Plop!

"I've seen some nasty campaigns in my day," Margaret Thatcher said as she leaned over to Helmut Kohl, "but this is the messiest affair the United States has ever produced. Half the crowd is splattered from this one."

When the bell sounded, marking the end to the event, the judges were unanimous that no winner could be declared because both contestants were covered with mud and muck beyond recognition.

The Fence Straddle has a long history as a political sport, but this was the first time it was sanctioned as an olympic event.

After a few steps, Quayle fell off the fence to the right, and Gore was unable to climb the thing. Bush gave a good performance until he started talking about the moderates in Iran and he also tumbled to the turf.

Clinton did a virtual ballet on the fence with the words, "I'm for a strong military posture including nuclear forces, as long as atomic power is not involved."

The Change-Horse-in-Mid-Stream competition was next on the slate of events, and the large crowd moved to the edge of their seats in anticipation of the action.

There was a hush over the throng as Clinton mounted his steed and galloped to the right shouting triumphantly, "I will not raise taxes on the middle class," but in mid-stream he switched horses with blinding speed as he whispered, "unless, of course, we need the money for my White House jogging track."

"Now that boy's got a real future in politics," Jerry Brown said to Ross Perot. "I've never seen any politician switch horses in mid-stream with that speed and finesse."

"Don't count ol' George out yet," Perot warned.

"No new taxes" Bush yelled as he sent the horse in full gallop up stream, but with blinding speed he switched horses and declared, "but the Democrats and the deficit might require it."

Rush Limbaugh dropped his microphone, and Republicans throughout the coliseum gasped in disbelief.

It was now time for the big event in the center of the coliseum. The Cow Chip Throw has long been a favorite in political campaigns; now it would take its proper place in olympic competition.

"I think the Republicans should toss elephant chips and the Democrats donkey chips," Democratic party chairman, Ron Brown suggested to Bill Bennett. "That way the event would have real symbolism."

"That suggestion really stinks, Ron," Bennett replied with irritation. "You know that elephants leave much larger...er...deposits than donkeys. We would be at a decided disadvantage."

"Ah'd lak t'be in this competition, too," Ross Perot shouted to the officials. "Ah been thowin' that stuff in Texas before Willie was even born."

"Sorry, Mr. Perot," Limbaugh replied. "There's a big difference between Washington beltway chips and the tiny bull chips you tossed in Texas. You've got to work up to the heavy stuff slowly. We don't want any political hernias at these games."

Clinton was first to throw. "I have always been for Star Wars research and development." Plop. "Wow, did you see that throw?" Dole said to Phil Gramm. "That's going to be tough for Bush to beat."

The large crowd was silent as a very calm and confident George Bush stepped into the ring and spun around with mind-boggling speed as he made his throw. "I am an environmentalist" he shouted. Splat!

Democrats slid down in their seats in utter disbelief. It was a gold medal performance without parallel. The Republican throng broke out in a wild celebration.

"Hey, there are five events yet to be contested and the stadium is almost dark," Limbaugh observed as the sun was beginning to dip below the horizon.

"That's no problem, Rush," Bush said poetically. "There are a thousand points of light out there."

And so the events continued well into the night, but without a clear victor.

As the exhausted crowd filed out of Kosciusko Olympic Stadium, we were able to see Bob Dole and George Mitchell walking arm in arm into a beautiful western sunset.

Warsaw may never be the same.

Off-Key Blue Jay

Tweet, Tweet And All That Stuff

It's a good thing blue jays are protected.

There's one in my backyard with laryngitis that insists on singing at the top of his lungs every morning at six. The sound is just frightful!

One blast of my shotgun could rid the neighborhood of that flea-bitten bag of feathers, but he knows I would end up in the hoosegow without bail for such a deed. So just about sunrise he arrogantly climbs to the limb nearest my bedroom window and belts out his rendition of the Barber of Seville.

"Why does he do that?" I keep asking myself. It can't possibly be romance; no self-respecting female jay would be caught dead with that nitwit.

With toothpicks holding my eyes open, I scanned my bird book at 6:05 a.m. yesterday morning and found to my amazement, that, romance, happiness or welcoming the sunrise have little to do with the music birds generate.

41

Most musical sounds produced by birds have far more serious functions, and these are generally relegated to three categories by ornithologists.

First, birds sing because they want to announce their presence in a given territory. Second, they sing to coordinate some activity with a mate, or third, their songs represent an aesthetic or emotional exercise.

Ornithologists refer to these primary songs as advertising, signalling and emotional.

But there is more.

Specialists have identified secondary songs such as the "whisper song" where birds repeat the notes of the primary song in much lower tones. Also, young birds are known to produce "rehearsal songs" as they work their way up to a full, adult repertoire.

Short, non-melodious sounds are often designed to warn other birds of danger, and these are designated "call notes."

Actually, bird songs can vary from species to species and be affected by location or the season of the year.

Things such as light intensity, weather and nesting practices can determine forms of singing. For instance, ornithologists have noted that singing increases during the nesting season.

Some birds have gained notoriety for the number of songs they sing in one day. Warblers, for example, can produce more than 1000 songs in a day.

The world record for singing, in case you wanted to know, belongs to a red-eyed vireo which produced 22,197 songs in one day! You might be tempted to conclude that what we have here is a very happy bird, but my bird-watching friend, Harvy Moot, says that in all likelihood, the bird was frightened by an intruder posing a threat to his home.

That mangy blue jay aside, the songs and sounds birds produce are really quite amazing. Some scholars have attempted to alter bird songs by cross-breeding certain types of birds, but not with any real success. My crazy uncle Hornripple once attempted to cross a parrot with a canary. He said he wanted a bird that could do both lyrics and music.

Given the opportunity, birds can get themselves into some wacky situations, also.

It was just a year ago when a blackbird broke into my neighbor's wine cellar. Hearing strange noises in my backyard at 3 a.m., I went out to check, only to find that bird hanging upside down from a tree branch singing "Melancholy Baby."

Of course, when it comes to singing, the canary is probably the champion for most people. While these feathered wonders produce a variety of songs for the owner, they are frail and rather difficult to protect. The following illustrates the point.

The story is told of a man who stormed over to his neighbor's yard where the owner was busy digging a hole. Pointing at a dead cat lying next to the hole he shouted, "What's the idea of burying my cat?" "I'm not burying your cat," said the man as he continued to dig. "I'm burying my canary, your cat just happens to be around him"

In case your wondering, I found a way to end the operatic renditions of that mangy blue jay outside my window. When he began his singing yesterday at 6:00 a.m., I piped a recording of Warsaw's mayor and Harry Caray singing, "Take Me Out to the Ball Game," to the to the tree limb on which he was perched.

I haven't seen the blue jay since.

A Bunny in Deep Trouble

Chickens Protest
Easter Tradition

There they were.

Colored eggs placed next to bunny rabbits on the store shelf. Easter is on the way, and stores everywhere are capturing the attention of children with their chocolate eggs and bunnies.

It all seems very innocent, doesn't it? That's what I thought until yesterday when chicken farmer, Dork Featherstone, paid me a visit.

"The hens have gone wild," a haggard Featherstone groaned as he stumbled through the door of my office. "They've left their nests and are picketing a rabbit hole out at the farm."

"We haven't gotten one egg in three days. I talked to one of the leghorns about the lack of production and all I got was a sarcastic, 'get a rabbit to lay your eggs,'" Featherstone explained as he brushed white feathers from his suit.

The usually calm general manager of Featherstone Egg Farm where one million chickens produce more

45

than 750,000 eggs a year, was visibly shaken by this unexpected uprising.

Fascinated by such unique chicken behavior and deeply curious as to why rabbits had become the object of their fury, I hustled out to the farm with Dork.

Sure enough, thousands of leghorns were strutting around with picket signs reading, "Down with Rabbits," "Easter is for Chickens," "Bunnies Unfair," and "No Recognition, No Eggs."

With pad and pencil in hand, I waded through hundreds of cackling hens in order to reach Lucy, chairhen of HUFFT (Hens United For Fair Treatment).

"What seems to be the trouble?" I asked, while sitting down on the ground in order to hear better.

"We're tired of all the publicity those miserable rabbits get every Easter season," she replied angrily. "Did you ever see a rabbit lay an egg?"

"Well, I make it a habit not to pry into the private lives of rabbits, or other wildlife, for that matter, but it's fair to say that rabbits don't lay eggs."

"Then tell me why all the attention is focused on those long-eared fleabags when it is we chickens who furnish all the eggs for the traditional egg hunts?"

"I'm not sure I can answer that," I admitted, "Perhaps, a rabbit could shed light on this dark mystery; so why don't we visit the rabbit hole being picketed?"

Followed by hundreds of mad hens, whose feathers were just bristling with fury, we approached the rabbit hole in the middle of the field.

A battered and weary bunny climbed out of the hole with some difficulty and protested, "Don't blame the rabbits. Blame the people of the ancient Near East for the rabbit and egg business."

"The Babylonians initiated a festival to be celebrated on the day of the spring equinox, with honors given to rabbits, who were symbols of fertility. Colored eggs were also employed to represent the bright light of spring and new life," he explained.

"We rabbits, of course, are into high-level reproduction, but that has never included eggs. Only the twisted minds of Homo Sapiens could concoct such ideas. So why don't you nutty hens return to your nests and let Featherstone get some sleep?"

It was very clear the hens were not about to buy what they perceived to be historical mumbo-jumbo, so the protest got larger and the clucking louder.

"Maybe you should see the Mayor of Warsaw," I suggested to Featherstone and Hiram Hackwood who had joined us in the pens. "After all, as a politician he's laid an egg or two in his day. Perhaps he could declare a 'Warsaw for Chickens Day,' or something."

"No, we shouldn't bother him," Hackwood responded with concern. "He's still recovering from the embarrassment of giving a fireside chat on television and having the fire fall asleep."

As we struggled to get back to the chicken houses, I turned to Lucy and suggested, "Why don't you get outside assistance for your cause? Colonel Sanders could be of help. He has a way with chickens, you know."

"Even for an outdoor writer, that's really tacky," Lucy snapped back.

"We deserve some respect from you humans, after all, we chickens have a long history of bailing the medical profession out of trouble. One can only guess how many of us have ended up in grandma's soup when someone in the family sneezed," she boasted. "We have earned our right to special honor."

Now Lucy was really getting into the picketing and protest mood. Standing on a tree stump she pointed her wing at me and asked, "Can you roost on a wooden peg while asleep and not fall to the floor?"

"Just look at Featherstone, there," she cackled. "He's never laid an egg in his life, yet he calls himself a chicken expert."

Thousands of irate hens voiced their approval of Lucy's observations.

"No question about it," I responded. "The hen is a marvelous exhibition of the Creator's skill, but when the bunny hopped into the Easter scene, he was there to stay. You hens might as well forget your strike and get back to work before you end up in a Breadings' Cigar Store Blue Plate Special."

"You know the old saying, 'An egg a day keeps the hatchet away.'"

I really felt that my compelling advice was so powerful that the hens would surrender and get back to production activities. Their fury, however, had now turned into uninhibited rage and they started toward me with blood in their eyes and picket signs in their wings. Never in my wildest dreams did I think I could clear a six-foot fence with a three step running start. Even now, my hands tremble just thinking about what one million mad hens could have done to my innocent body.

Chickens are very dangerous creatures.

Now, for The Weather

Weather Watch

"Well, it looks like we've got some rain coming our way today," Quigley Hornberger said to me as we sat on the city bench in front of Breadings' Cigar Store.

"How do you figure that?" I wanted to know. "The sky is clear today."

"This cup of coffee is the key. When bubbles bunch up around the edges of your cup, it means the atmospheric pressure is low, thus indicating an impending storm," he explained.

"Look at my cup. Bubbles are all around the edge. If the bubbles were all in the center, it would mean the day is going to be fair."

"I sure wouldn't depend on Breadings' coffee to predict anything except heartburn by 11," I responded skeptically. "When the inspector from the Environmental Protection Agency visited this place and examined the food and coffee, he declared the joint a toxic waste dump."

But ol' Quigley was not about to change his mind. You see, he depends on beaver tails, wooleybear caterpillars, horse hair, and squirrel nests to get a handle on winter weather.

Never mind that modern weather bureaus have the latest in hygrometers, satellites, computers, barographs, psychrometers and humidistats.

"According to a study conducted by the National Center for Atmospheric Research in Boulder, Colorado, most long-range forecasters are right only 60 percent of the time," Quigley argued. "Give me two minutes with a horse in October, and I'll improve the forecast by 20 percent."

Conventional wisdom says that if the hair on a horse is long, it's going to be a bad winter. Also, squirrels are thought to grow bushier tails in preparation for a harsh season.

"The real telltale sign for this winter was Fillmore's coat," Quigley announced.

"Who in the world is Fillmore, and what could his coat possibly have to do with the weather?"

"Fillmore is a woolybear caterpillar who lives in the bush next to my kitchen window. When that reddish-brown stripe down his body is narrow and dark, it's going to be a bad winter. Count on it," he explained. "Fillmore's stripe is narrow and dark."

"There are two more signs of a severe winter that have never failed me. The early departure of ducks and the tough skins on onions."

"Surely you remember that weather-wise poem,
  Onion skins very thin,
  Mild winter coming in.
  Onion skins very tough,
  Winter's coming cold and rough."

"The ducks on my lake left two weeks earlier this

fall, and the onion skins on the hamburger Burleigh Burgh cooked for me yesterday were as tough as a doormat," Quigley noted with finality.

"I sure hate to burst your bubble, but the word 'tough' applies to everything Burgh cooks."

Snow depth and the severity of winter storms, according to local sages, are reliably reflected in the height of hornet nests and the behavior of hogs.

> See how high the hornet's nest,
> 'Twill tell how high the snow will rest.
> When pigs carry sticks,
> The clouds will play tricks.

I had to admit that the weather was surprisingly cold this week, and Wednesday's snowflakes provided some excitement. It was so cold on Tuesday night that the residents at Grace Village Retirement Center had their electric blankets in overdrive all night!

"But what about winter colds? How do you cope with those irritating things?" I was anxious to learn.

"Nooooo problem," Quigley answered. "Eat plenty of chicken and chicken soup. It'll cure you in no time flat."

"I sure hate to be so reluctant to grab onto these gems, Quigley, but I don't believe I'm convinced on that one."

"Just think about it, John. When was the last time you saw a chicken sneeze?"

He had me there.

"I always like to recommend my mother's' Prune Elixir for fall colds," Quigley quipped. "You mix one half a glass of prune juice with one half a glass of fig juice."

"Sorry, but I just don't see how that mixture could cure a cold," I argued.

"Well, it doesn't exactly cure the cold, but it makes you think twice about coughing."

The Farmer's almanac is forecasting more snow this year, but I'm not sure that I want to stake very much on that prediction or that of my TV weatherman with all his gadgets.

I guess when you get down to it, there's nothing really as reliable for weather forecasting as the aches and pains in my arthritic knee.

A Slim and Trim Santa

Keep Santa Fat

I could hardly believe my eyes.

As Santa ended his slide down my chimney, he landed in a heap among the ashes, and his toys scattered everywhere.

"This job is really the pits," he grumbled. "There's got to be a better way of making a living."

Standing in front of me in a sagging, torn red suit was a man who could not have weighed more than 135 pounds.

"What in the world happened, Santa?" I wanted to know."I stayed up tonight expecting a plump, happy ol' Saint Nick, and all I get is a skinny grouch covered with soot."

"Look sport, the last thing I need is some inane observations from a sleazy outdoor writer," he snapped with irritation.

Possessing the keen analytical mind that I do, I immediately noticed that something was awry here.

57

First, Santa was only a skinny echo of the man whose belly usually shook like a bowl full of jelly, and second, the "ho, ho,ho's" were gone completely.

There was a story here and I was going to get it, grouchy Santa or no grouchy Santa.

"Santa," I said politely, "I couldn't help noticing that you have dropped quite a bit of weight since I saw you last Christmas. Was this Mrs. Claus's idea?"

"No, Maggie made me do it," he responded.

"Maggie?"

"Yes, Margaret Stutzman who runs Warsaw's weight loss center. Last year she refused to let me enter her house, arguing that my physical image and habits were downright disgraceful and she would have nothing to do with perpetuating them."

"Then she told Mrs. Claus that if I would follow her Belly and Bottom Buster diet plan, I could have a really swell body when I visited Warsaw next year."

"The next thing I know this diet plan arrives in the North Pole, and since then it has been nothing but alfalfa, celery, broccoli, carrots, cauliflower and exercise."

"I'd like to see you sit down to dinner after eight hours of hard work with the elves and have a couple of sprigs of parsley, two crackers, some grapefruit rinds and a steamed bluegill stare back at you. It tends to take the 'ho, ho, ho's' out of your vocabulary," Santa continued.

"It got so bad that one day I snuck out to the barn and snatched some oats and sugar cubes away from Donner and Blitzen," he explained while brushing the soot off his suit.

"Has this new body format helped you in your Santa activities this winter?" I asked.

"Having a swell, slim body has been nothing but frustration," he noted with despair.

"When I made my annual appearance at Wilson's Department Store, children cried and mothers shouted insults at me."

"I can't smoke a pipe any longer so I have taken up chewing gum. I'm up to ten packs a day."

"Wow, you really have had a rough year," I said sympathetically.

"Oh, that's not the half of it. I went into Breadings' Cigar Store and got mugged by some toothless geriatrics playing dominoes. Boy, were they mad."

"Well, that's easy to explain," I said. "Last year the old guys asked you for a new cook, and when they returned on the 26th, there was Burleigh Burgh burning the eggs again."

The last time I saw Santa this depressed was when he was fined by the Federal Aviaton Authority for not having air bags on his sled.

I had to do something to correct this whole distorted scene. "How could Margaret do this to little kids and the grand traditions of the yuletide season?" I asked myself.

It seems to me that Stutzman, Jane Fonda and Richard Simmons are part of a national conspiracy to make America skinny and dull. Have you ever noticed how bored ants are? They're all the same size and shape...no lumps, curves or flab. That's why they always show up at your picnic. They're bored to tears looking at their perfectly shaped bodies and enjoy looking at yours.

"Santa," I said with appropriate authority, "Magaret and Mrs. Claus have got to realize you can't mess with tradition. A skinny, gum-chewing St. Nick is not going to make it."

"The world expects a paunchy philanthropist bouncing down their chimney at Christmas time, not an inferior shadow of him."

Now, I was really getting mad and began to pace the floor with Santa.

"The kids of Warsaw deserve a real Santa. A fat Santa. A happy Santa," I shouted while punctuating the air with my fist. "Margaret has no business monkeying with Santa's belly."

Santa's eyes regained a little twinkle, and he lifted his head as he paced the floor with me.

"Just look at the outstanding people who gave obesity a sense of greatness: Alfred Hitchcock, Robert Benchley, Robert Morley, Orson Welles, Charles Laughton, Peter Ustinov, Winston Churchill, Jackie Gleason, Babe Ruth, Tommy Lasorda, Andy Devine, Margaret Dumont, Sydney Greenstreet, Ethel Waters, Oliver Hardy, Marie Dressler, and Buddha."

"Winston Churchill without his cigar and 275 pounds? World War II would never have been the same," I declared.

"Well, I guess I never thought of it that way," Santa said as he popped a piece of chocolate in his mouth.

"Of course I'm right," I shouted with ministerial authority. "Just look at the mess thin people have gotten themselves and our world into. There's Hitler, Yassir Arafat, Billy Martin, Attila the Hun, Tokyo Rose, Caligula, Jim Bakker, and Burleigh Burgh."

"Onward obesity, forward with flab and higher with heavyweights," Santa barked while munching on a piece of pizza. The spring had returned to his step; he lit up his pipe and started to put toys under the tree.

It will probably take a year to regain his full,

Christmas stature, but he was well on the way.

Please, Margaret, trim down the ol' scribe if you must, but keep Santa fat!

The Great Debate

Now, What Was That You Said?

When I was young and cutting my teeth on soft pretzels and Italian hoagies, I used to visit the Bronx Zoo in New York City.

Not any more.

You now enter the gates of the "International Wildlife Conservation Park" if you want to see exotic birds or snakes.

It seems that the word "zoo" has taken on so many negative nuances, that a politically correct name change was called for. After all, when you hear people describe Ft. Wayne's largest shopping mall as being a "zoo" on a Friday nights, you know the term is not complimentary.

On the same grounds, it would appear that in the near future "jungle," "welfare," "gay," "lobby," and "closet" will all eventually be given quiet burials.

According to the loud and liberal left, all segments of our language must be revised to conform with politically correct thinking and speaking. In fact, one man recently objected to my using the expression "politically correct words" and suggested that I refer to them as "adverbially premodified adjectival lexical units."

This critic also made it clear he no longer wanted to be referred to as "bald," but rather as "hair disadvantaged" or "follicularly challenged."

If all this lexical pressure for political correctness doesn't have your head spinning, untangling the code language in our newspapers surely will. A recent "personal" ad in a regional paper, for example, read, "Guy of average height and looks, who is progressive-thinking and good-natured, desires a relationship with a lady."

According to my good friend Gardenia Hucklemeyer, that ad really meant he was, "Ugly as a pygmy rhino, would do dishes and laundry without any nagging, and did not want to marry."

Last winter I was standing in front of Breadings' Cigar Store soaking up some culture when Florescent Farleft and her daughter came walking by. Florescent is not exactly a charming conversationalist, but without anything else to do, I decided to engage her in a little small talk.

"Hi, Florescent. Say, your little girl, Magnolia, is really growing up," I said warmly to open conversation.

"Magnolia is not a little girl, she is a prewoman," she snapped back with icy contempt. "In fact, in just four years she will be a freshperson at Purdue University where she will be majoring in herstory."

Now, friends, we outdoor writers might not be psychological whizzes, but we do know when the needles are up on the porcupine, so I chose a topic I was sure she could respond to in less testy tones.

"I was glad to read that the police arrested that crook who had been burglarizing your neighborhood. He was really a bad egg," I noted.

"Look, you verbal slob, that distressed person was not an evil crook, but just someone who was morally different," she responded angrily. "Can't you get anything straight?"

"Look John, I can't waste my time here in idle and idiotic chatter," she continued. "I've got to get home so I can water my botanical companions and help Magnolia make a snowhuman in the front yard." And with that, she and her prewoman marched off, careful not to fall into an open personnel access structure in the street.

It was not long before Arnie Axlerod, a ninth-grade teacher in Fogbottom Middle School, came cruising by and it was clear he was very depressed.

"Hi Arnie," I said cheerfully. "What's up?"

"I don't know what's going on these days," he said glumly. "It seems everything I say is wrong."

"This morning I had a parent's meeting with Florescent Farleft about the disruptive class behavior of her little gir...er prewoman, Magnolia."

"Her indignant response was, 'My daughter is not a disruptive child. She is merely a prewoman with an attention deficit disorder. All preadults engage in negative attention-getting at one time or another.'"

"I thought I was done with the political correctness lectures for the day when our librarian sent back my book order with the word 'book' crossed out and 'processed tree carcass' written in," he added.

"I hear people talking these days," Arnie groaned, "but I don't have the foggiest idea what they're saying."

All this corrective verbal action had me deeply confused, so I decided to wander into Warsaw's only center for cultural sanity and verbal stability. . . Breadings' Cigar Store.

"Hi Burleigh. How's the ol' cook? Say, I really like that after shave you're wearing," I noted with proper charm.

"Sir, I am not a cook," he barked back. "I am a highly refined culinary artist who is wearing a quality discretionary fragrance, and I serve only the best in fleshburgers with botanical accompaniments."

I couldn't believe my ears. "Burleigh Burgh into things politically correct? Please say it isn't so!" I said to Bill Backlash who was sitting at his table feeling as stunned as I was.

"Burleigh, did you hear that lazy Fred Foose lost his job with the street department again?" I asked in hopes of more normal conversation.

"John, Fred did not fail and lose his job. That's a politically insensitive statement. He is merely a motivationally dispossessed individual with temporarily unmet objectives," he responded with professorial authority.

By now I was really semantically depressed, but it got even worse when attorney Phil Harris ordered two stolen nonhuman animal products scrambled with brutalized and browned botanical matter.

Clouds of deep despair drifted around me as I rambled to the bench outside. In just seconds, Solomon Sunflower, an angry animal activist marched up and objected vociferously to a hunting article I had just published. "You're nothing but a stupid outdoor writer," he concluded.

That did it.

No longer was I going to be anybody's lexical

doormat or the innocent victim of verbal cannibalism. With a mixture of professional pride and righteous anger I shouted, "I strongly object to any language that labels this scribe a stupid outdoor writer."

"I am a mentally disadvantaged wildlife wordsmith and don't you forget it!"

It Actually Tastes Like Chicken

It Doesn't
Taste Like Fish

Imagine my surprise when I walked into a Toledo restaurant and, after ordering a catfish dinner, was greeted with, "Sir, you're going to like that dinner; it doesn't taste like fish."

Now, according to my culinary expectations, one usually orders fish because it feels like fish and tastes like fish.

"Ma'am, if this catfish doesn't taste like fish, what exactly does it taste like?"

"Well, it tastes like fish, but it isn't fishy. Y'know, it's sorta like very mild chicken."

That explanation was not helpful for the simple reason that I'm not sure I know what chicken tastes like anymore.

Chickens are now raised in a grit-free environment; and fattened with grain that is enriched with vitamins, proteins, anti-biotic chemicals, and fast-growth hormones.

When the chickens arrive at the restaurant, they

are marinated for three days in exotic sauces, then coated with 13 herbs and spices, and finally covered with a one-inch layer of flavored bread crumbs.

The chef, a bubble-gum chewing teen-ager, plops them into three-day-old grease and then giggles with his girlfriend over the counter while that magnificent fowl is singed beyond recognition.

The whole issue here is really quite simple. I dragged my taste buds into this Toledo, waterfront restaurant to enjoy an advertised catfish special that tasted like catfish.

So I pressed on.

"Is there any chance, then, I could order some chicken and get closer to the taste of catfish? You see, I really do enjoy the taste of catfish. Somehow when I bite into catfish and it tastes like chicken, the fun is gone."

"What are you, some kind of nut?" she asked with a twinge of irritation. "Nobody likes the taste of fish. That's why so many people eat chicken."

She was right, of course. Americans have a passion for tasteless fish and the commercial fish packaging industry has made millions of dollars catering to those culinary desires.

"I think I have an answer to our problem," I said with enthusiasm. "Why don't you just serve me some of your fried perch and when you bring it in, say, 'I hope you enjoy your catfish?'"

"You wouldn't like that," she said with apprehension. "Our perch doesn't have a very fishy taste. It is sorta like a mild veal taste. The public just loves it."

"Well, is there any chance your veal tastes like perch? I'll just skip the idea of catfish and settle for the taste of perch."

"Look, sport, if you really want something that tastes fishy, you'll have to get our crab salad," she informed me.

"That's funny, I always thought the public liked crab meat because it was mild-tasting, not really fishy."

"Not here in Toledo," she announced with pride.

For the shallow of mind, insensitive of heart and dull of taste bud, resolving this fish dinner crisis might seem like a futile engagement with the inconsequential.

But vital culinary and piscatorial traditions were at stake here, so I persisted in my search for something that tasted fishy.

"Ma'am, is there any chance this "blackened fish" on the menu would come close to the taste of catfish?"

"That might be your best bet," she responded."When our chef blackens anything, you can assign whatever taste to it you wish and you won't be far off. I'll call it catfish, you call it catfish, and then we can wrap this whole thing up so I can go home."

When the dish arrived, a square, black coated something or other laid there in the middle of the plate. When I took my first bite, the 47 spices mixed with chimney soot took my breath away and made my eyes water.

I'm not sure, but I think I drank a 16 ounce glass of water in world record time.

With a devilish smile on her face, the waitress looked at me and said, "y'see, when you really get down to it, a catfish does not taste like a cat and hamburger does not taste like ham, does it?"

She had me there.

A Majestic City Symbol

Warsaw's
Official Fish

Have you noticed how depressed the people of Warsaw have been recently?

After an extensive investigation that left no lily pads unturned, I was amazed to discover that the doldrums have been produced by a lack of an official city fish. The fine citizens of this city are growing in sophistication and want to be on the cutting edge of cultural advancement.

Of course, I recognized this trend more than a year ago and pleaded with the city fathers to make the majestic asparagus the official city vegetable. Our Mayor and the City Common Council snubbed my suggestion and our fair town has been slipping into cultural obscurity ever since.

Here we sit with three lakes surrounding us with more than 900 acres of water, not to mention the Tippecanoe River and numerous private ponds, and we have no official city fish.

I ask you, where is our piscatorial pride?

Even the state of Illinois recognized the importance of having an official fish, so they conducted an election among the elementary school children of the state and (to nobody's surprise) the bluegill won.

Now, I have been informed that the state of Hawaii has made a similar move. After holding elections at the Waikiki Aquarium, the Humuhumu became the official fish of the state.

The Humuhumu, a figure in early Hawaiian legends, is known for its strategy of swimming into a small crack and using a special spine to lock itself in place, preventing other fish from extracting and eating it. The Humuhumu will serve as the state fish for five years, after which it must run for re-election.

If Illinois and Hawaii can have official fish, why not Warsaw? Do we have to wait for the tiny towns of Claypool, Packerton and Leesburg to lead the way again?

Wanting to get a handle on what species would make a good candidate for Warsaw's official fish, I went to the city's cultural and intellectual center, Breadings' Cigar Store (at, I might add, great risk to both stomach and nervous system).

"What fish do you think Warsaw should adopt as its official symbol?" I asked Filbert Fern who was attempting to stab his fried egg as it floated in a small pond of brown grease.

"That's easy," he snapped back. "The largemouth bass is the only fish worthy of such an honor." I should have expected that answer from a guy with 63 fishing product patches on his jacket.

"No way the bass should get the nod," Henry Hornripple barked back. "The bluegill or crappie should adorn the flag flying over city hall. They outnumber those dumb bass by ten to one."

Sensing widespread conflict on this issue, I turned to the wizard of wit and the guru of gossip, Breadings' chef Burleigh Burgh. The whole joint turned graveyard silent, and customers leaned forward to hear Warsaw's only five-star chef speak.

"The carp should be Warsaw's official fish," he announced in authoritative tones.

Half the customers rolled on the floor laughing, and snickers could be heard from people passing by the food emporium at the time.

As much as I hate to admit it, he was right.

Trout anglers are probably gagging at the very thought of a carp on Warsaw's official flag, but let me remind the snob set that the fly fishermen's patron saint, Izaak Walton, called it "queen of the rivers; a stately, a good, and a very subtle fish."

Walton thought so highly of the carp that he included a whole chapter on them in his classic, *The Compleat Angler*, first published in 1653.

For years the carp has been an expensive and a highly prized fare on European menus.

Let's face it, gang, there isn't a fish cruising our lakes that grows any bigger and endures more punishment than that golden beauty. Just ask Department of Natural Resources biologists, Jed Pearson and Ed Braun. They have poisoned the poor devils, drained lakes and employed every modern technique to rid our waters of the carp, but without success.

In a short time, the carp returns and resumes rolling in the muck with unbridled glee.

When Warsaw's lakes are polluted, causing bass, bluegills, crappies and channel catfish to rise to the surface belly-up, the carp will be gliding through the sludge like nothing happened.

No doubt about it, the carp is here to stay.

Fishing for the carp is highly recommended by heart specialists because it fights like an old shoe and will not cause high strung anglers to blow a gasket when one is on the line.

Mayor, here's your chance to make a real mark in Indiana politics. Forget sewer hook-ups, park expansion, athletic complexes, road widening and airport improvements. That's minor league stuff.

Name the carp as Warsaw's official fish and anglers worldwide will face our city and salute.

Santa's New Image

Santa, A Republican?

I couldn't believe my eyes!

There was beardless Santa Claus sitting in his traditional chair at the department store dressed in a dark pinstriped suit.

He had a calculator in one hand and with his other he held a child on his bony knee. This Santa could not have weighed more than 180 pounds.

Next to him was an elf sitting at an IBM PS2 with a spreadsheet on the screen.

Worse yet, some little children had actually left his knee crying. I wasn't able to take it any longer. Being a fearless outdoor reporter, I just had to investigate this matter.

"Santa," I shouted with appropriate journalistic authority. "Never in my life have I seen you dressed like a Madison Avenue yuppy, sending children away crying. What's going on here?"

"Look, Mac, my working agenda for today does not list an interview with a sleazy outdoor writer. If you have questions, you'll have to make an appointment with my secretary and go through a written pre-screening test just like these kids," he responded in a high squeaky voice.

"I have permission from Waldo Hornripple, the store manager, to talk to you and he's paying your salary," I responded with some irritation.

"Ok, ok, I guess I can grant you a few minutes. I've taken on a new image to conform better with the realities of American life," he explained. "The promotion of a fat old man with a scraggly beard and a vocabulary equal to a rock provides a very poor role-model for young people in a highly competitive economic environment."

"No longer do we allow kids to come with a wish-list and then promise them the world. That giveaway mentality fostered by liberal, bleeding-heart Democrats has got to end. This is the era of Reagonomic sanity."

"But these little kids have worked hard to be good all year, and they look forward to being rewarded for that kind of behavior," I noted.

"Good does not count anymore," Santa asserted. "That is an outmoded ethical notion that only violates good business principles. What really counts is productivity. If kids cannot show a net profit of at least ten percent from their weekly allowances, they can't get in line, sit on my knee and order a new year's supply of floppy disks."

Now I was furious.

"You mean we'll never hear that jovial 'ho,ho,ho' with a belly shaking like a bowl full of jelly, again?" I asked with outrage in my voice.

"Ho,ho,ho is out," Santa barked back. "Such inane banter does not create a good business environment. What kids really need to hear is 'downside risk,' 'bull market,' 'bottom line,' 'cost containment,' and 'market feasibility.'"

"I suppose that the traditions of a sled, reindeer and night delivery are also out?" I asked in depressed tones.

"You got that right," Santa replied. 'The Society for the Prevention of Cruelty to Deer' put an end to the use of deer and OSHA impounded my sleigh because it did not have tail lights, a windshield, seat belts, and air bags. I'm glad, too. Frankly, I was weary of freezing my tail off delivering gifts in bitter cold December temperatures."

"There is some good news, though," Santa quipped with his first smile. "OSHA has agreed to release my sleigh and overlook the legal problems with using deer if I will agree to make a few late night military equipment deliveries to Iraq. They informed me that the amount of money I would be receiving from Swiss banks would be quite handsome."

"They also promised that I would not have to file a flight plan with the FAA, and none of the baggage would be X-rayed."

A little girl got up on Santa's lap after the elf checked her year-end investment performance. Before she could say anything Santa asked, "Did you send your Christmas requisition form X10-1772 to me by December 1st with the original and two carbons as required by North Pole Delivery Ordinance 331?"

The little girl hadn't. Heartbroken, she tearfully ran into her mother's arms.

Santa was unmoved by the whole affair. "Kids have got to learn responsibility sometime," he grumbled. "It's a nasty world out there."

With a break in the line, Santa took out a cigar and

lit up. As puffs of smoke rose to the ceiling, I asked why he was not smoking a pipe as tradition requires.

"Creates the wrong image," he replied. "Everybody knows that cigars are symbols of success. Look at George Burns, Danny Thomas and Winston Churchill, to name just a few."

"Do you intend to do away with traditional Christmas music as well?" I wanted to know.

"You betcha. 'All I Want for Christmas is My Two Front Teeth, encourages a deficient values system; 'I'm Dreaming of a White Christmas' has racial overtones; and 'I Saw Mommy Kissing Santa Claus,' encourages hygienically dangerous behavior patterns.

"But don't conclude that we've done away with Christmas music altogether," Santa assured me. "The new music will just be more economically and socially relevant for our day. Just wait 'till you hear 'Money and Mistletoe,' 'Portfolio Polka,' 'Bank Street Blues,' 'I'm Dreaming of Black Ink,' and 'Wall Street Winter.'"

"You may also be interested in knowing that since my workshop at the North Pole is too geographically isolated and too costly to heat, I am relocating it in California's Silicon Valley. Furthermore, elves have not proved to be highly skilled laborers, so we're going to the U.S. Congress to recruit some new workers. Why, some of the people in that place can actually read and write."

Never in my 20 years of investigative reporting have I been more depressed by an interview. Christmas will never be the same.

Santa, a Republican yuppy?

Please, tell me it isn't so!

ofFISHAL INDIANA STATE FOSSIL BALLOT

(select one)

☐ **1.**

DIPLODOCUS ULTRASAURUS
(DIPLODOCUS)

☐ **2.**

ISOTELUS GIGAS
(INDIANA TRILOBITE)

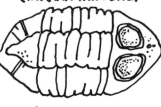

☐ **3.**

MAMMUT AMERICANUS
(MASTODON)

✗ **4.**

HOMOSAPIEN REPUBLICANUS
(JEAN NORTHENOR)

I'M REPUBLICAN

A Very Logical Choice

State Fossil

Now I'm really depressed.

First, it was the city of Warsaw languishing in social insignificance, now I have learned that our glorious state floats in the backwash of intellectual sophistication.

For years I have fought valiantly to have Warsaw adopt an official fish (carp), vegetable (asparagus) and insect (cockroach). In spite of my devastating logic and irrefutable factual information, Mayor Jeff Plank and the city Common Council apparently slept through their chances to put Warsaw on the map.

As a result, our city continues to lack meaningful symbols of greatness and cultural significance, and a depression hovers over the place like an eerie fog.

Now, it has come to my attention that Indiana, the 12th largest state, does not even have an official fossil.

Why, even such insignificant and culturally

backward states as New York, Pennsylvania and California have adopted state fossils.

In fact, 14 states now proudly display an official fossil in their state buildings including lowly Idaho (the hagerman horse), Montana (the duck-billed dinosaur) and Kentucky (the brachiopod).

How would you like to be one of our fine Warsaw elementary school teachers or principals on a field trip to the State building. Hovering over your cherubs you might say, "Look children, here are some very special state symbols. The peony is our state flower, the cardinal is the official bird and the tulip poplar the state tree."

"Over here you will see the state song, poem and stone," you would announce with appropriate pride. But some student recognizing the glaring cultural oversight will undoubtedly ask, " Teacher, where is our official state fossil?"

I can just see the embarrassment and humiliation on your face. What can you possibly say to that student to explain why Indiana has failed to find a fitting fossil to evoke its prehistoric past?! Oh, the shame of it all!

As a conscientious and dedicated outdoor writer committed to Hoosier greatness, I cannot sit idly by and allow Indiana to slip further back into cultural oblivion.

After weighing the normal available resources on this portentous issue, I decided to pay a visit to that hot-bed of scientific and philosophical intellectualism—Breadings' Cigar Store.

I hit chef Burleigh Burgh's emporium of gastronomic calamities at noon, and the joint was just teeming with intellectual dialogue. At every table sophisticated thinkers were elucidating highfalutin' concepts of philosophy, annotating the conclusions of geology, illustrating the conundrums of theology and prognosticating all the calculations of eschatology.

It was awesome except for two intellectual perverts at the back table who insisted on talking about St. Louis Cardinals baseball.

I spotted Studs Hornripple, Mike Mildew, and Dork Goodflat at a table and joined them. "Studs," I asked, "if you could pick an official state fossil, what would it be?"

"That's easy," he responded with paleontological conviction. "It has to be that great representative of the family, Titanosaurideae: the Diplodocus. This gigantic herbivorous dinosaur attained lengths of 85 feet and is one of the most significant finds in the Upper Jurassic sediments of Montana. It fed mainly on aquatic vegetation and lived around swampy lakes. Since our state has many lakes, it only makes sense that this would be Indiana's official fossil."

"You're goofy," Dork Goodflat blurted out. "That reptilia is not even found in Indiana. Most remains have been located in the west. The only legitimate fossil for our state is the Indiana Trilobite. "

"It is common to Indiana Devonian and Silurian rocks of the Paleozoic period and only grew to two or three inches. It's small enough so that kids could wear them on necklaces and bracelets."

"It would be a scientific tragedy if this extinct marine arthropod would be overlooked," he concluded.

"That's sheer nonsense," Mike Mildew bellowed. "That tiny fossil is totally unimpressive and certainly not zoologically significant. The only real candidate can be the mighty Mammut Americanus or American

Mastodon."

Breadings' was now engulfed in total silence as these intellectual powers continued debating this complex issue.

Mike Mildew proceeded, "This massive mammal stood nearly nine feet high at the shoulder, had rusty brown hair and each foot had five toes. Indiana must have an official fossil that's majestic and paleontologically significant."

But with every proposal there was widespread dissent among the scholars who had gathered for Burgh's Desert Storm Special—hump of camel. There was nothing resembling a consensus in that haven of heartburn, so I decided to wander off to the shore of Pike Lake and do some heavy pondering.

"I can't ask state representatives to vote on something geologically insignificant," I said to myself. "The official state fossil—above all—must be really old, well-known, noticeably decrepit and politically correct."

Then, like a lightning bolt out of the sky, an absolutely brilliant solution flashed across my troubled mind.

I raced back to Breadings' where the debate continued at a fever pitch. Standing in the doorway, I shouted, "I've got it! The perfect candidate for the official state fossil!"

A solemn hush came over the place, and all eyes were glued on the ol' scribe.

"We've all agreed this fossil has to be really old, unbelievably decrepit, a survivor of the ravages of time and, in addition to all that, politically correct, haven't we?" I asked.

All the intellectuals nodded their heads in agreement.

"Well, I know an aged senior vice president at Lake City Bank who is a bit dilapidated, but fits all the qualifications of our prehistoric relic. Since she is the Margaret Thatcher of Indiana Republican politics, we could call her, Homosapien Republicanus. Gentlemen, the only logical choice for the official state fossil is none other than Jean Northenor."

Thunderous applause broke out, and with great relief, the Breadings' philosophers shouted approval.

I sat down and sipped coffee as I basked in the glow of one of the few really significant triumphs of my life. But the experience was short-lived.

Suddenly I came to the sobering realization that I would be the one who would have to inform her of this great honor. How could I tell Jean and keep her from tearing my tender body into a thousand pieces?

Life can really be cruel at times.

The Ol' Scribe Listens *Very* Carefully

It's A Matter of Image

"We're sick of the shabby image we've been given and we're going to do something about it," a deep voice growled at me from the far end of the picnic table.

Up to that moment, our trip to Yellowstone National Park had been an experience of calm, gentle breezes and breathtaking scenery.

Startled, I whirled around only to find myself staring into the bloodshot eyes of a giant black bear. To say he was angry would have been the understatement of the century.

My inclination was to look for the nearest tree and make like a squirrel, but my usually slow brain sent a split second reminder that he could climb trees better than I could.

"Sit down," he growled with authority as my knees pounded out a rhythm worthy of a Latin band. "You either hear me out or you're history," he growled while his giant claws slashed at the air to refine his demand.

As an outdoor writer with a keen sense of observation, I have learned not to ignore reasonable requests, especially when they are couched in such crisp, direct language!

"What exactly is it that has ruffled your fur?" I asked with appropriate politeness, not even requesting an explanation of how he learned to speak English.

"The heart of the matter is image. We're fed up with the rotten image bears get in cartoons, stories and sports," he grumbled. "We bears have pride and don't appreciate constantly being portrayed as zoological buffoons with the intelligence of a rock."

"Every Saturday morning millions of kids park themselves in front of the television set and what do they see? Yogi Bear hopping around in a silly hat, stealing lunches and driving park rangers into mental hysteria."

"Kids conclude that we spend all of our time robbing innocent tourists because we don't have the intelligence to find our own food. Actually, we have one of the most wide-ranging diets in the world and will eat practically anything that is chewable including animal rights protesters. Our preferences are fawns—yes, Bambi included—weak mammals, mice, ground squirrels, frogs and even small birds."

"In the summer we catch migrating fish in the streams, and in the fall we collect berries, pine cones, and seeds," he continued.

"Then, there is Smokey the Bear who wears a ranger's hat and gives everyone reminders not to burn the place down, but does it with all the charm of a flat tire. I've had more excitement watching rust form on tractors," he mumbled with obvious irritation.

"Well, what message would you like me to take back to Warsaw regarding your image?" I asked.

"Look at the claws on my paws, the muscles in my body and my razor-sharp teeth. We're majestic creatures full of power, intelligence and the ability to survive in any environment," he confidently answered.

"We're tired of being portrayed as teddy bears, honey bears or even Russian bears. The film, *Bad News Bears* with Walter Matthau is an insult to our species. How could Walter get tied in with a bunch of brats pretending to be a baseball team, and then allow the bears to be their name?" he asked with bewilderment.

"I also want you to know that we're not too thrilled with that Chicago circus act known as the Cubs, either. Why people pay to watch grown men run around in knickers and lose game after game is beyond me."

"Well, I'm confident bears are more accurately portrayed in literature than on television or in the movies," I suggested hoping that he would calm down.

"Oh, sure we are," he responded with biting sarcasm. "Take that classic piece of nonsense entitled, Goldilocks and the Three Bears. Now there's a real cultural gem."

"Three bears living in a house is bad enough, but preparing hot cereal for breakfast is enough to make my nails curl."

"Here are three real sharp yahoos. They go for a walk in the woods and leave their front door unlocked. When they return, it takes them 20 minutes of searching a one-room house to find Goldilocks sleeping in the small bed. Worst of all, they let her escape!"

"That book should have been banned from the IU and Purdue curriculums years ago out of respect for the dignity of the polar, brown, black, sloth, spectacle and sun bears," he shouted with anger.

The giant black bear was now pacing up and down in front of the picnic table, punctuating his remarks with slaps of his paw which sent wood chips flying in every direction.

"The ultimate insult is to have an NFL football team named after you that exhibits all the finesse of an elephant on ice skates," he roared. "If we caught salmon like the Chicago Bears catch passes, we would starve. It's the only team in the NFL that has an offense built around a humpback and three drawbacks."

"Do you know what it's like to be in your den reading about the Bears getting torn up by Falcons, clobbered by Eagles, battered by Rams, crushed by Colts, slaughtered by Lions, squashed by Seahawks and pounded by Dolphins?"

"Sure, the Chicago Bears have had a rough season," I observed, "but the coach has promised a modernized version of the team next year. That should restore your pride and reduce post-game drinking by the fans."

"Modernizing the current Chicago Bears is like painting racing stripes on arthritic camels," he responded sarcastically.

"Well, surely there is some likeness between Yellowstone's wild bears and the Chicago Bears," I suggested.

"Of course there is," he responded. "We both hibernate through the winter months."

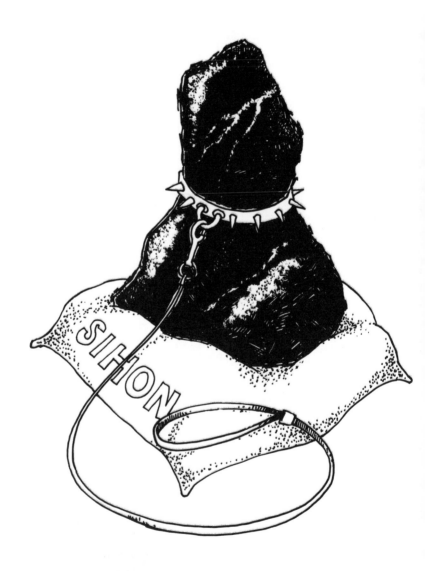

World's Greatest Pet

The Perfect Pet

Finding the perfect pet is not easy.

Dogs bark, cats scratch, fish die, parakeets molt their feathers all over the place and horses are too expensive.

After a long and arduous search throughout the animal kingdom, which was reinforced by my years of archaeological field experience, I've concluded that the best domestic pet is a rock.

When I saw my wife putting newspaper under our cuckoo clock a couple of years ago, I knew any pet we had in the house would have to be squeaky clean. A rock is clean.

But there are other advantages as well. Rocks come in all sizes, shapes, colors and weights. They are durable and consume no food whatsoever. There is an air of dignity and mystery that surrounds rocks as is evidenced by the enthusiasm geologists display in studying them. So valuable are they in providing information on the history of the universe, the United States government has spent millions of dollars to get some from the moon.

My pet rock is very special since I brought him back in 1976 from the land of Jordan where I had been excavating. His name is Sihon and he is made of basalt, a black, volcanic stone.

Filled with enthusiasm, I marched into the kitchen for lunch and announced that Sihon was now an official member of the family.

"Your new pet is a what?" my wife responded with a combination of amazement and disbelief. "Have you stripped all your mental gears?"

"Not at all. In fact this is the most meaningful pet I have had to date," I responded with cool confidence.

"Basing my conclusion on hard experience I have deduced that rocks are alive." I explained. "They not only grow, but they creep."

"Remember last year when I camped out in the Bob Marshal Wilderness in Montana? I cleared the whole area of stones and rocks so I could enjoy a good night's sleep. Halfway through the night I awoke with a rock directly under my back."

"Three times I moved my sleeping bag and each time stones and rocks ended up beneath me. I know scientists say that rocks come to the surface as the result of freezing and thawing, but no veteran camper would ever buy that theory."

"Just park your sleeping bag anywhere and stones will find a way to get under it. They must be lonely," I offered.

"Would you like mustard on your hot dog?" my wife inquired, totally ignoring the devastating power of my arguments. "Or perhaps you would like it with rock salt, today."

I refused to be discouraged by such a callous

display of sarcasm and shifted my arguments to the prestige of rocks.

"Surely, you're aware that from our earliest years rocks play a critical role in our lives. What mother has not sung "Rock-a-bye Baby" to a crying infant?"

"A rock is the most impressive pet available to the American public today," I announced. "The Rocky Mountains were named after them, and so was one of Notre Dame's greatest coaches—Knute Rockne."

"A rock speaks of wealth," I continued. "Who can forget the vast fortunes of J.D. Rockefeller? People spend years developing rock gardens.

"When the astronauts soared into space, remember, it was a rocket that got them there. Rocks speak of peace and comfort. That's why one of the most popular chairs is called a rocking chair. Surely, these facts give pet rocks some stature," I demanded.

"Would you care for any more coffee or potato salad?" she asked with cold detachment from the whole discussion.

"Look, rocks are so significant they have become a part of the language of big investors on Wall Street. Just the other day I heard Achish Featherbelt say that all his stocks had hit rock bottom."

"Rocks are the biggest thing going with teenagers today. I know that some say "grass" is their bag, but have you ever noticed how many go to rock concerts?"

"Furthermore, rocks speak of strength and power as evidenced by the fact that five films have been made portraying the life and times of a boxer named Rocky."

"Well, all those arguments are interesting," my wife quipped with patronizing tones, "but what can they do?"

"Glad you asked that," I responded with renewed vigor. "Take my incredible Weather Rock, for example. All you have to do is suspend it in the air on a stand, take it outside, and it will tell you all sorts of interesting things about the weather."

"If the rock casts a shadow, it is sunny; if it collects dust, it is calm; if it swings, it is windy; if it is wet, it is raining; if it is white, it is snowing; if it is horizontal, there is a hurricane; if it jumps up and down, an earthquake has hit; and finally, if it disappears, a tornado went through. "

"John, would you hand me the phone book?" my wife asked in subdued tones.

"Aha! My arguments on behalf of Sihon the rock have overwhelmed you and you want the phone number of the pet shop to cancel your order for a parrot," I responded with glee.

"No, I'm calling Warsaw psychiatrist, Dr. Millard Graymatter, to make an appointment for you. Frankly, I don't think you have both oars in the water anymore."

"I don't quite know how to tell you this," my wife continued. "But if Sihon was that black, ugly rock on the dresser, he was given a Hefty Bag burial at 9 a.m. I was collecting leaves this morning and needed some weight to keep the bag from blowing down the street, so I slipped the rock in with the leaves. You will be glad to know that Sihon did an admirable job."

My heart sank. I had hauled that rock 7,000 miles from Jordan only to have it end up in the bottom of a Hefty Bag in the city dump.

"Isn't there any rock that you like?" I asked in depressed tones.

"Well, there is that great Russian pianist, composer

and conductor—Rachmaninov."

Duck Hunting Blues

Duck Hunters' Alibis

You know it's going to happen.

Barney Farnsworth will carefully plan his duck hunting outing for weeks. He will clean his $400 Browning, select the right shells, pack his new plastic decoys for travel, tuck a new Sure Shot triple reed duck call in the top pocket of his camouflage suit, and give his boots a complete waterproofing.

Three days and a large motel bill later, he will slither through the back door of his home with an empty game bag.

As always, Mom and the six kids standing in the kitchen will ask in unison, "How many ducks did you get, Daddy?"

Poor Barney will only be able to stand there, lonelier than Madelyn Murray O'Hair at a convention of Methodist Bishops, and painfully admit his failure.

I know the feeling well.

More than once Daffy Duck and his friends have quacked their way past my 12 gauge pump gun. This is embarrassing enough, but having to explain it all to skeptical family members and neighbors is downright humiliating.

Therefore, through the years I have developed a solid collection of duck hunting alibis for just such occasions. Here are a few of them.

1. The tide was out — the ducks refused to land in the mud.
2. The tide was in — there was so much water, the ducks were scattered all over the lake.
3. There were too many weeds on the water — I couldn't find the ducks in the vegetation.
4. There weren't enough weeds on the water — all the ducks landed in another lake for their salad.
5. Kinky bass fishermen were speeding around in their $25,000 boats looking for one more pre-sunset hot spot.
6. The Canadians must have shot all the ducks before they started south.
7. The Department of Natural Resources wouldn't let us go where the ducks really were.
8. DNR Fish biologists Ed Braun and Stu Shipman must have collected all the duck eggs along with the fish last spring.
9. The sky was too clear — the ducks stayed too high to shoot.
10. The sky was too cloudy — the ducks landed and hid before we got there.
11. There weren't enough hunters along the river to keep the ducks moving.
12. There were too many hunters along the river, and they scared the ducks clear out of the county.

13. The steel shot I was using must have been rusty — it didn't carry far enough.
14. The boat ramp was ice covered — my car slid into the water, and it took four hours to get it out.
15. I must have gotten an old box of shells — my shots kept falling behind the ducks.
16. I must have gotten some new overloaded shells — my shots kept nipping their bills, but not one duck fell.
17. The duck blind was too big — I couldn't hide.
18. The duck blind was too small — I fell into the water when I turned to shoot.
19. My hunting partner was too noisy.
20. The ducks never made a pass at the decoys except when I had my glasses off to clean away the frost.
21. My 10 gauge, 48-inch barrel shotgun just isn't big enough. I need a new gun.
22. My 10 gauge, 48-inch barrel shotgun is too big. When I finally get it up in the air, the ducks are in the next county.
23. It was too windy — the ducks were flying too low.
24. It was too calm — the ducks were flying too high.
25. The ducks were all so small I didn't have the heart to shoot them.

Well, there you have it. Of course, there are hundreds of other alibis in use around our county produced by very creative (and desperate) hunters.

So, Barney Farnsworth, wherever you are, cheer up. You may not have a duck after the hunt, but a snappy alibi will prevent the depressing humiliation that is sending more and more hunters to psychotherapists.

Party Time in The Woods

Groundhog
Wisdom

Groundhog Day has gotten out of hand.

First, it was only Punxsutawney Phil who was pursued by information-hungry weather watchers longing to learn the length of winter; now we have a whole army of pretenders.

There is General Lee (Snellville, Ga.), Chipper (Chicago, Ill.), Chuckles (Manchester, Conn.), Jimmy (Sun Prairie, Wis.), Melvin (Greensboro, N.C.), Octorara Orphie (Quarryville, Pa.), French Creek Fredie (French Creek, W. Va.), Dave (Dunkirk, N.Y.), Tilly (Tacoma, Wash.), Woodrow (West Orange, N.J.) and Willie (Wiarton, Ontario, Canada).

Did you notice something disturbing about the above list? All the great and progressive cities in our country and Canada are represented except for Warsaw, Indiana.

I was really depressed over that and again wondered what our mayor and city council do at all those meetings they have.

107

We have a fire department, police department, street department, even a snow drift inspector, but no official groundhog we can consult for reliable winter planning.

Must our fair city continue to be relegated to the ranks of the obscure and backward? Will we continue to depend on the shallow and unreliable speculations of television weatherpeople and their shaky analysis of weather station data for our information?

In a sincere effort to fill this talent gap in Warsaw's government, I went south of the city to the woods where that overstuffed rodent, Clyde the Groundhog, lives.

I wasn't exactly thrilled with the prospect of waking that cantankerous animal up again on Feb.2, since all my previous attempts had been exercises in verbal futility.

But he's the only talking groundhog in the city I knew, so I decided to pay him a visit.

"Hey, Clyde," I shouted down in his hole. "Are you awake? It's Feb. 2nd again."

I really expected a thoroughly grouchy face to appear as it has the past ten years, but to my utter surprise, Clyde had a bow tie on and was brushing confetti off his shoulder as he emerged with a bright smile.

"Hi, John, I sorta expected you along sometime this morning. Phew! Last night was really something out here in the woods!" he noted with a twinkle in his eye.

"I don't understand. I thought you and the other animals were in hibernation and would have been sound asleep."

"Not on your life," Clyde explained. "Ever since the Kosciusko County Council closed down the

animal control services, it's been one continuous
party here in the woods. I think every dog, cat and
pet skunk must have been out here dancing into the
wee hours of the morning."

"The air was filled with romance. Let me tell you,
John m'boy, when litters start appearing this spring,
Warsaw residents are in for a surprise or two."

"You mean that here in the woods you had food,
entertainment and all that?" I asked in disbelief.

"Yep. Ol' Doc McCleary was out here with his
electric organ favoring us with such animal classics
as 'Old Mcdonald Had a Farm,' 'How Much Is That
Doggie in the Window?' and 'Lassie, I Love You.'"

"Burleigh Burgh, Warsaw's King of Cholesterol,
prepared his famous Soybean Souffle. You see, we
animals take a dim view of eating each other at such
festive gatherings, so we stick to vegetables."

"Well, that's all very interesting," I noted, "but I
came out here to see if you would be willing to have
Mayor Jeff Plank appoint you as Warsaw's official
groundhog and weather prognosticator. It's just too
expensive for us to run back and forth to
Punxsutawney, Pennsylvania."

"Sorry, John, I'm not into weather anymore. I've
left Center Street for Wall Street and graduated from
the supermarket to the stockmarket. Stocks are where
the action is."

"That's too bad, Clyde."

"Say, there are at least 50 to 60 educated
groundhogs that live in the city limits; do you think
any of them would be willing to accept the
appointment?" I wanted to know.

"I don't think so. Melvin, for example, has decided
he doesn't want to work anymore, so he's going to be
a college professor. Sidney enjoys public popularity,

so he's accepted a school superintendent's job; and Barney wants to make bundles of money, so he's applied for an outdoor writer's job."

"Hey, I've got a great idea," Clyde gurgled with enthusiasm. "Why don't you have Rob O'Brian, president of the Chamber of Commerce, dress up like a ground hog for Feb. 2. He would cast a very impressive shadow and be able to promote the city at the same time.

"No, that wouldn't work," I responded with deep disappointment and despair. "There's no tradition for Chamber of Commerce types casting shadows and predicting weather. If we attempted to pass off a 5' 11", 175-pound groundhog to the press, we would become the laughingstock of the state."

I just couldn't bear the thought of Warsaw going another decade without it's own official groundhog. So I pressed on.

"Surely there's a groundhog somewhere that would be willing to work for the city in this very strategic position. Can you tell me where I might start looking?"

"Oh, I dunno," Clyde responded thoughtfully. "You might try the United States Congress. Most everybody there hibernates during the winter and when they are awake, they spend most of their time predicting and promising."

It's A Matter of Perspective

I Didn't
Shoot Bambi

"How could you shoot Bambi?" Fred Flatbottom asked in testy tones as he looked at a mounted deer head in my study.

"I didn't shoot Bambi, I shot a male deer for food under strict rules designed to protect the herd. It's not possible to shoot Bambi, because Bambi doesn't exist," I replied.

"If Walt Disney says there's a Bambi, there's a Bambi and that's that," he concluded with noticeable conviction.

I decided not to pursue this line of discussion because dinner was about ready, and I wanted to preserve a congenial atmosphere.

However, his unexpected outburst does underscore the power of the theater. The Walt Disney animated classic has had a profound effect on many who now see all deer as Bambis dancing merrily though unspoiled forests and meadows.

The emotional impact of Bambi, from the opening strains of "Love is a Song That Never Ends" to the vision of Bambi and his father standing on a cliff at the end, is powerful.

While the film, Bambi, is interesting entertainment, it is also bad biology.

Forests are made out to be havens of perfect serenity as all animals and birds dance and sing together to the accompaniment of hundreds of violins.

The truth of the matter is, forests are violent stages on which the drama of survival is played out. Foxes eat rabbits, hawks swoop down on little birdies, snakes snatch eggs before the young can be born and wolves prey on innocent grouse.

The magic of the Disney production has distorted the real issues of conservation and game harvesting with the result that a whole generation of baby boomers thinks every animal has big eyes with fluttering eyelashes.

The dynamic of anthropomorphism and anthropopathism through animation has produced a generation of "animal rightists" who would risk a human at a drop of a hat in order to protect an owl.

Anthropomorphism, in case you may have forgotten, is the attribution of human behavior or physical characteristics to animals, inanimate objects or natural phenomena. Anthropopathism, on the other hand, ascribes to inanimate objects, animals or natural phenomena human emotions or sensibilities.

Bambi is filled with human-like love scenes that have animals fluttering their eyelids at each other and kissing. In more than 40 years in the woods, I have yet to see a doe flutter her eyelids to get a buck excited or a pair of skunks kissing.

In the film the "girls" nearly always have big blue

eyes that flutter and drop the boys in their tracks. Now, at our local cigar store I have seen the male of the species fall off his chair when a passing blond winks, but out in the woods a groundhog is not known for his "smooching" techniques.

Don't mistake my assessment of this grand film epic; it is still great entertainment. However, to enjoy it you do need to overlook the biological errors, which are numerous.

For example, animals don't make friends with each other; in all probability, Friend Owl would eat Thumper and Flower if he got the chance. The closest to reality that Friend Owl comes is when the birds disturb him in the early spring with their singing and he responds with the musical refrain, "They are a Pain in the Pin Feathers."

Male deer do not raise their young or take over if their mate dies. Bambi and Faleen make a nice fictitious couple, but in reality, deer do not pair off to raise a family. Bucks will mate with many does during rut.

When you see Bambi in mid-winter with spots and a baby-like appearance, you know the artist was a city boy. By winter most fawns lose their spots and take on a more adult-like appearance. No less than three times, hunting is introduced in the film and always in powerfully charged emotional settings. Shots ring out in the spring (there is no deer hunting then, of course) and in the fall. Perhaps the most interesting hunting scene occurs when hunters are portrayed shooting everything in sight and unleashing a whole pack of dogs to run down the deer.

No one argues that there aren't some first class slobs in the hunting fraternity, but most hunters are thoughtful sportsmen and women.

The whole issue came into clear focus during the dinner with Fred Flatbottom. Fred, president of PCA ("Protect Cute Animals"), and I were enjoying the meal and the beautiful lake-front view from our dining room. There was laughter and joking, but my heart was heavy.

I watched as he stuck his fork into the roast beef. "That," I said to myself, "is a terrible way to treat Benny Bovine, who was undoubtedly somebody's father. He probably had big brown eyes and danced innocently across the pastures, never hurting anyone."

Then Fred snatched up a couple of spears of asparagus. "Just think," I said painfully, "only weeks ago that little asparagus was soaking up the sun while waving joyfully in the Indiana breezes. Somebody came along and sliced that innocent plant bringing its carefree existence to an end, just to feed a grouchy member of the PCA."

The tossed salad with its sacrificial remains of lettuce, carrots and tomatoes was also a grim reminder of the brutality of man at his worst.

I couldn't restrain myself any longer.

"Fred," I said with deep passion, "how could you eat that beautiful cow whose big brown eyes once gazed innocently over the rolling hills of the farm and peacefully ate the tender green grass of serene meadows?"

"Tender vegetables who attacked no one, you have devoured with emotionless efficiency. Oh, how utterly painful all this is!"

Catching the logic of my questions he responded with equal gusto, "long live Bambi!"

Somehow, I get the impression this debate is

going to be with us for a while.

One Gift Too Many

The Romantic Outdoorsman

Christmas is the season for memories, gifts, romance and creativity.

My friend and avid outdoorsman, Hiram Hackwood, desired to do something special for his wife since he had been away so much during the past year on fishing and hunting excursions.

He decided to make this Christmas uniquely different and more reflective of the great traditions that surround this, the most important of holidays.

He meandered into one of Warsaw's large department stores on the first day of Christmas, and the conversation went something like this....

"Now let me get this straight," the gray-haired clerk said. "You want a partridge and a pear tree along with two turtledoves sent to your wife, Rosebud, during the next two days? Does it matter if we box the partridge and the turtledoves separately?"

"Yes, it does matter," Hiram replied resolutely. "The partridge must be in the pear tree, and the

doves cannot be delivered until the second day of
Christmas. Details are important."

"Oh, Hiram," Rosebud gurgled as she met at the
door upon his return from work. "How perfectly
original and sweet! The gifts arrived and I've put the
partridge and the pear tree in the living room. It is a
real conversation piece. Our neighbor, Barney
Bimwell, is building a pen for the turtledoves. You
are a darling."

The next few days were not easy for our Romeo.
Pet shops, novelty stores and garden centers turned
deaf ears to his requests for French hens, calling
birds and geese a-laying. Finally, he decided to
return to the department store where he had
purchased the first gifts.

"Now, look, Hiram," the old clerk groaned. "I
know the store policy is to get whatever a customer
needs for Christmas gifts, but I'm only a year away
from retirement and the joy of my benefits. This
nutty project of yours could cost me my job."

"The five golden rings are no problem, and the
pet division says it can come up with four calling
birds in addition to three French hens, but where in
the name of Nimitz do you think we're going to find
six pregnant geese in the middle of winter? How
about six fat parakeets? They make great pets, you
know."

"No deal," Hiram responded. "It's going to be six
geese a-laying or I'm complaining to the manager.
Christmas tradition and literary accuracy are at stake
here. The one thing I did learn at Fogbottom
University was how to read Christmas music."

Later on over a candlelight dinner at the Hot 'n
Now burger shop Rosebud reflected on the gifts of
the week. "Hiram dear, the five golden rings were

delightful, but the French hens have pecked most of the feathers off the turtledoves, and the four calling birds have kept our neighbors awake for a whole week."

"Also, eating six goose eggs every morning is a bit of a chore even when they're used in omelets. Maybe, we ought to be thinking of more contemporary-type gifts, don't you agree?"

"Not on your life. We outdoorsmen thrive on the unusual and the dramatic. Believe me, the charm of this British approach to honoring you, my love, will be one of your most cherished Christmas memories," he explained with an angler's confidence and optimism.

The sight of Hiram Hackwood cruising down the aisle toward the special gifts department was no moment of joy for the old clerk. He had just concluded a two-hour go-around with Warsaw's leading tightwad, Bill Chapel, who insisted that there was a Chanel No.4 and it was a lot cheaper than the No. 5.

"Now look, Hackwood. I got your telephone order for seven swans a-swimming, eight maids a-milking and nine ladies dancing and if you don't mind a purely personal evaluation, I think you're a kook. Why me? I've worked here for 31 years and have enjoyed every Christmas."

"I just spent three hours on the phone attempting to uphold our store's good name by filling this order. Swans I can get, but the only way they're going to do any swimming is if Winona Lake doesn't freeze over."

"Our manager, Harvy Fern, came up with the eight cows, but getting eight maids to milk them in this cold weather is another matter."

"I checked every dance studio within 100 miles,

and there isn't one that has nine female, English dancers. I called Dork Featherstone, and he said the best he could do was nine disco dancers from Madam Fifi's Night Spot in Claypool. You'll have to settle for them."

"Hello, Hiram?" Rosebud shouted over the phone. "Have you lost your marbles all together? The swans are eating the neighbor's bluegills, and the cows are making a mess on the lawn. During the church ladies' auxiliary meeting at our home this afternoon, the disco dancers appeared and created total bedlam. The pastor plans to review our membership."

"If I get one more crate of birds or another herd of cows, you can plan on sleeping in the garage the next four weeks."

"I just don't understand it," Hiram said with dejection after the phone call. "I've spent more than $5,000 on these unique gifts which just drip with old-country tradition. Maybe Rosebud is upset because the set is incomplete. That's it! Now, let's see," he reasoned with renewed enthusiasm. "On the 10th day, 10 lords a-leaping, 11 pipers piping on the next day and 12 drummers drumming on the final day. Wow! When Rosebud gets these terrific gifts and sees the complete picture, she will be ecstatic."

"You want what?" the old man groaned after hearing Hiram's latest order. "Say, this wife of yours has quite a sense of humor, doesn't she? I mean, my wife would have had me committed to Harry's Happy Farm by now or at least arranged for a quick check-up by our local shrink, Dr. Millard Graymatter."

"Look, lover boy, I'm going to need some time to get this order together. Why don't you come back tomorrow and if I'm not fired by then, I might have the gifts." The next day brought good news to our romantic fisherman. "I have everything you asked for, but with some slight modifications," the rapidly aging clerk explained. "I couldn't locate 10 lords a-leaping, but Mayor Jeff Plank said the city council was a little on the flabby side, so he is sending them to your home to hop around the yard a few days for conditioning."

"Melvin Mossback and Barry Bushrack agreed to provide the pipers, but insisted that all 12 drummers be allowed to bring their own trap sets."

Hiram's business office phone rang again.

"Hello Bozo," a very frustrated and angry Rosebud began. "What's the big idea? The Conservation Department is investigating the illegal entrapment of wild animals, the SPCA and the Humane Society have filed suit for cruelty to animals, and every time the disco dancers do their thing, our neighbor, Mr. Hornripple, calls the police."

"The drummers sent the cows running through the neighborhood, the pipers are off-key and those leaping councilmen are ruining all the flower beds."

"Our bulldog, Rover, is on the verge of a complete nervous breakdown and is undergoing therapy with Dr. Hornberger at the animal shelter."

"Endless noise, flying feathers and the disco dancers are driving me crazy. If you really love me, you'll bring a broom, mop, and a big shovel and clean up our house. These have been the 12 worst days of my life! I'm on my way to the Harry's Happy Farm for my first treatment, so don't contact me for a few days."

Deeply depressed and bewildered, Hiram Hackwood left his office and sat on the curb in front of the building. Drifting snowflakes landed softly on his head as he stared into space.

"I guess my fishing buddy, Hector Lebble, was right after all," he mumbled. "Maybe, I need to be more practical at Christmas. He got his wife a tackle box and a year's subscription to *Hoosier Outdoors Magazine* for her Christmas gift. Now, why didn't I think of that?"